Examberry

Advanced Level Vocabulary
Book 3

CW01497442

So, why learn vocabulary?

The simplest answer is that as human beings, our most common means of communication is language. It is through the use of language that we express our ideas, needs and emotions. Words are the building blocks we use to share our intelligence. Having a greater number of words allows us to communicate with each other in ever more elaborate, sophisticated and persuasive ways.

On a more mundane level, expanding vocabulary is vital for children sitting 11+ grammar and independent school entrance exams. In both types of exam there is an element of creative or descriptive writing in which examiners are specifically looking for evidence of a well-developed vocabulary.

An extensive vocabulary suggests a child is well and widely read and able to put forward ideas and arguments in an intelligent way that will be helpful in all areas of academic life, not just in English language lessons.

The most natural way to increase a child's vocabulary is through reading a wide variety of books. That way a child can pick up new words while seeing them used in context. However, this involves years of enthusiastic reading and not all children are natural bookworms.

If your child is not a great lover of reading, this book will help expose them to new words and the exercises included with each vocabulary list will encourage your child to use these words, in context, in real sentences.

As they work through the list you can support your child's learning by encouraging them to use the newly acquired words in everyday speech, perhaps when describing their day, an incident at school, or a favourite film. As your child begins to use these previously unfamiliar words they will become more confident about using them in their work and their expressive writing skills will quickly develop.

Contents

Vocabulary 1

Learn the words below and then answer the questions that follow!

1. **Analyse** (v.): to examine, inspect, look closely at.
   The teacher asked us to **analyse** a poem by exploring the techniques used by the poet and the emotions conveyed.

2. **Mandatory** (adj.): required by law, compulsory, obligatory.
   It is **mandatory** to wear a helmet when riding a motorbike.

3. **Secondary** (adj.): coming after (second); subordinate, less important than.
   The town has two **secondary** schools for pupils aged between 11 and 18, as well as three primary schools for younger children.

4. **Eligible** (adj.): meeting the conditions to do something, permitted, entitled.
   As a student, Susan was **eligible** for a 20% discount at the university cafe.

5. **Replenish** (v.): to fill something up again, recharge, reload.
   An efficient waiter will **replenish** your glass as soon as it is empty.

6. **Pitiless** (adj.): showing no mercy, cruel, heartless.
   The **pitiless** king slaughtered those who disobeyed his commands without even hearing their pleas.

7. **Malignant** (adj.): evil, spiteful, cancerous (of a disease), deadly or harmful.
   Dutch elm disease is a **malignant** fungal disease spread by bark beetles, which has wiped out many elm trees in the UK.

8. **Nausea** (n.): feeling of sickness, discomfort, queasiness.
   Carl had a dreadful feeling of **nausea** in his stomach after the rollercoaster ride.

9. **Morale** (n.): spirit or mood, confidence, self-esteem.
   After losing in the final, the tennis player's **morale** was very low and he felt he should give up the game for good.

10. **Conservatory** (n.): a room with a glass roof and walls, attached to a house and often used for displaying plants; glasshouse for plants.
    Our new home has a **conservatory** with views over the garden.

27/4

Exercise A: Synonyms

Write the word from the vocab list which is *most similar* in meaning next to each word listed below.

1. Mood — Morale
2. Recharge — Replenish
3. Entitled — Mandatory
4. Glasshouse — Conservatory
5. Obligatory — eligible
6. Subordinate — Secondary
7. Heartless — Pitiless
8. Sickness — Nausea
9. Examine — Analyse
10. Evil — Malignant

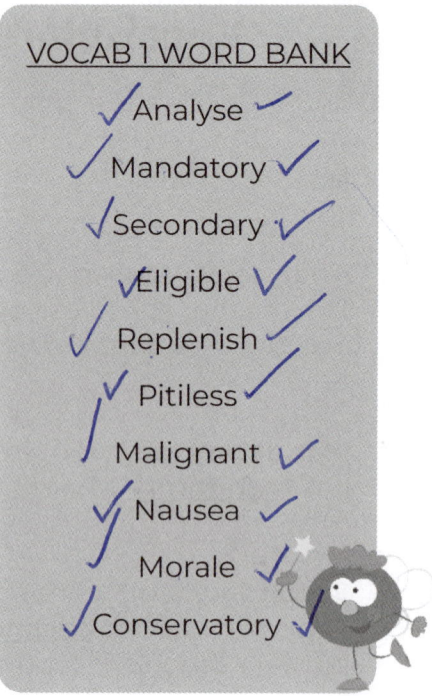

VOCAB 1 WORD BANK
- ✓ Analyse ✓
- ✓ Mandatory ✓
- ✓ Secondary ✓
- ✓ Eligible ✓
- ✓ Replenish ✓
- ✓ Pitiless ✓
- ✓ Malignant ✓
- ✓ Nausea ✓
- ✓ Morale ✓
- ✓ Conservatory ✓

Exercise B: Complete the sentence

Write the most suitable word from the vocab list in the spaces below. You might need to change the form of the word; for instance, walk might become walked.

1. It is _Mandatory_ to pass your driving theory exam before you take your driving test.
2. The pirates treated their prisoners with _pitiless_ cruelty by making them walk the plank one by one.
3. Jason was overcome with _Nausea_ as the boat rocked from side to side.
4. Our _Morale_ was very high after we won first prize for our group project.
5. The author donated many new books to _replenish_ the shelves of our school library.
6. My netball coach _analyse_s our matches carefully to help us improve our tactics.
7. The farmer's primary source of income was from his cows, whereas his small herd of goats was of _Secondary_ importance.
8. Only citizens over the age of eighteen are _eligible_ to vote in elections.
9. Aunt Liz had a _malignant_ tumour in her lung, but doctors were able to remove it.
10. I want to grow some new, exotic vegetables in our _Conservatory_.

Exercise C: Complete the sentence

Select the most suitable word from the choices provided.

1. Only the students on full-time courses are _____ to apply for a loan.

   a. replenish　　　b. eligible　　　c. malignant

2. The exhausted, hungry soldiers spent the winter in freezing conditions, and as a result their _____ was very low.

   a. morale　　　b. mandatory　　　c. pitiless

3. The pharmacist recommended tablets that would _____ my calcium levels.

   a. nausea　　　b. replenish　　　c. conservatory

4. Ayesha was told that the painkillers could cause _____ and fatigue.

   a. secondary　　　b. analyse　　　c. nausea

5. The headmaster reminded students that proper uniform was _____.

   a. mandatory　　　b. malignant　　　c. pitiless

6. Having collected the data, the students carefully _____d the results.

   a. replenish　　　b. morale　　　c. analyse

7. Winning the tournament is of _____ importance; it is the participation that really matters.

   a. malignant　　　b. secondary　　　c. conservatory

8. The witch punished the frog with a _____ glare, which turned him to stone.

   a. nausea　　　b. mandatory　　　c. malignant

9. The dictator's regime was _____ and caused great misery to his people.

   a. pitiless　　　b. analyse　　　c. secondary

10. My favourite _____ at Kew Gardens contains a vast collection of cacti.

    a. morale　　　b. mandatory　　　c. conservatory

Vocabulary 2

Learn the words below and then answer the questions that follow!

1. **Parable** (n.): a story with a moral message, a teaching.
   The **parable** of the 'Good Samaritan' from the Bible encourages us to treat everyone equally.

2. **Inquest** (n.): official investigation, inquiry (into the cause of death), review of a case.
   An **inquest** is always held if murder is suspected.

3. **Indignation** (n.): anger at unfair treatment, resentment, annoyance.
   When Barry's flight was cancelled for no apparent reason, he was filled with **indignation**.

4. **Feasible** (adj.): likely, probable, achievable, realistic.
   Arriving at the party before 8pm was only **feasible** if James left work on time.

5. **Esteem** (n.): high regard, admiration, approval, respect.
   Louise is held in high **esteem** by all her colleagues, who value her advice.

6. **Aromatic** (adj.): pleasant smell, fragrant, perfumed.
   Zoe's kitchen is often filled with the **aromatic** scent of exotic spices that she loves to cook with.

7. **Flippant** (adj.): disrespectful, thoughtless, dismissive.
   The Prime Minister was criticised for his **flippant** tone when discussing the serious issue of homelessness in the UK.

8. **Sympathise** (v.): to pity, commiserate, express sorrow for someone's misfortunes.
   I **sympathised** with Elyse after she broke her arm, as I could see she was in pain.

9. **Incessant** (adj.): continuing without pause or interruption, constant, endless.
   My dad was driven crazy by my **incessant** drumming sessions in the basement.

10. **Cumbersome** (adj.): awkward, weighty, inconvenient.
    Hannah found her skis heavy and **cumbersome** when she had to carry them from the hotel to the ski slope.

Exercise A: Synonyms

Write the word from the vocab list which is *most similar* in meaning next to each word listed below.

1. Admiration _esteem_
2. Disrespectful _flippant_
3. Constant _incessant_
4. Story _parable_
5. Achievable _feasible_
6. Pity _sympathise_
7. Awkward _cumbersome_
8. Resentment _indignation_
9. Investigation _inquest_
10. Fragrant _Aromatic_

VOCAB 2 WORD BANK

Parable
Inquest
Indignation
Feasible
Esteem
Aromatic
Flippant
Sympathise
Incessant
Cumbersome

Exercise B: Complete the sentence

Write the most suitable word from the vocab list in the spaces below. You might need to change the form of the word; for instance, walk might become walked.

1. Marcus felt a mixture of self-pity and _indignation_ when he was picked last for the gymnastics squad.

2. Tilly was exhausted by her baby brother's _incessant_ crying every night.

3. In the future it may be _feasible_ for humans to live on the Moon.

4. Although the tractor looked _cumbersome_, it was easy to drive.

5. Lewis wanted to be held in the same high _esteem_ as his successful brother.

6. Mum put _Aromatic_ eucalyptus oil onto a handkerchief to help unblock my nose.

7. In our Religious Studies lesson at school, we studied some of Jesus's most famous _parable_s.

8. An _inquest_ was held after the rock band's plane crashed in the desert.

9. The teacher was furious with Sam's cheeky and _flippant_ answers.

10. Even though Anjum supported Liverpool, she could _sympathise_ with the Chelsea team because they had so many injuries.

Exercise C: Complete the sentence

Select the most suitable word from the choices provided.

1. Martin's new bath bombs were both _____ and colourful.

   a. inquest   **b. aromatic**   **c. esteem**

2. Millie could barely carry the rucksack as it was so heavy and _____.

   a. incessant   **b. indignation**   **c. cumbersome**

3. _____s can help us to understand abstract ideas, such as morality and justice.

   a. parable   **b. sympathise**   **c. flippant**

4. Mum asked our builder if it was _____ to finish the loft conversion by Christmas.

   a. esteem   **b. aromatic**   **c. feasible**

5. Everyone _____d with Carla when her pen ran out of ink in the exam.

   a. indignation   **b. sympathise**   **c. parable**

6. Despite my _____ pestering, Dad refused to take the family to Thorpe Park.

   a. incessant   **b. inquest**   **c. cumbersome**

7. We were snowed in again over the weekend, to our great _____.

   a. flippant   **b. indignation**   **c. aromatic**

8. The actor Leonardo DiCaprio is held in high _____ and has won many awards.

   a. sympathise   **b. esteem**   **c. feasible**

9. There was an _____ into the deaths of several passengers after the bus crashed.

   a. inquest   **b. aromatic**   **c. cumbersome**

10. Jake takes a _____ attitude towards the dangers of riding a motorbike, so he never wears a helmet.

    a. flippant   **b. esteem**   **c. incessant**

Vocabulary 3

Learn the words below and then answer the questions that follow!

1. **Trite** (adj.): boring due to being overused; dull, overdone, unoriginal.
    The plotline was so obvious that many critics called the film **trite** and predictable.

2. **Stipulate** (v.): to demand a requirement, specify, instruct.
    The rules **stipulate** that students must not wear jewellery to school, without exception.

3. **Delectable** (adj.): delicious, flavoursome, mouth-watering.
    My grandmother's cookies are so **delectable** that it is difficult to stop eating them.

4. **Definite** (adj.): clearly stated or decided, fixed, certain.
    Madge said that her parents had **definite** plans to move abroad next year.

5. **Thrifty** (adj.): using money and other resources carefully; frugal, economical.
    Beth was a **thrifty** student, only buying clothes from second-hand shops.

6. **Replete** (adj.): to be completely full of, brimful, bursting with.
    The report was **replete** with errors and therefore had to be rewritten.

7. **Interject** (v.): to say something abruptly, interrupt, cut in.
    Cameron would not wait his turn and tried to **interject** when Amy was speaking.

8. **Hospitality** (n.): welcoming and looking after guests or visitors, friendliness, generosity.
    I wrote to thank the Shao family for their warm **hospitality** during my recent stay with them.

9. **Administration** (n.): management; organisation or running of a business.
    The **administration** is looking at how to cut costs and protect the future of the company.

10. **Jeopardise** (v.): to put at risk, threaten, endanger.
    My teacher told me I would **jeopardise** my chance of getting a high grade if I handed my essay in late.

Exercise A: Synonyms

Write the word from the vocab list which is *most similar* in meaning next to each word listed below.

1. Interrupt ___interject___
2. Brimful ___replete___
3. Unoriginal ___trite___
4. Threaten ___jeopardise___
5. Management ___administration___
6. Generosity ___hospitality___
7. Economical ___thrifty___
8. Specify ___stipulate___
9. Delicious ___delectable___
10. Certain ___definite___

Exercise B: Complete the sentence

Write the most suitable word from the vocab list in the spaces below. You might need to change the form of the word; for instance, walk might become walked.

1. The restaurant had outstanding reviews for its ___delectable___ food and excellent service.

2. The inhabitants of the remote island voted to remain under the ___administration___ of the French government.

3. I had to ___interject___ when Phoebe began listing incorrect facts and information.

4. Marco was a ___thrifty___ shopper and collected coupons to save more money.

5. The basketball players' contracts ___stipulate___ that they must attend all training sessions and games.

6. My travel plans are not ___definite___; I still haven't booked any flights.

7. Jonah's attempt to sound intelligent came across as ___trite___ and silly.

8. Marcela took a risky decision that could ___jeopardise___ her whole career.

9. It is an important part of many cultures to show generous ___hospitality___ to guests.

10. The fridge was ___replete___ with snacks after Mum and I went to the supermarket.

Exercise C: Complete the sentence

Select the most suitable word from the choices provided.

1. The contract _____s that you must work for the company for a minimum of three months before you can take a holiday.

   a. replete   **b. definite**   **c. stipulate** ✓

2. The police urged members of the public not to _____ their lives by driving during the hurricane.

   a. hospitality   **b. jeopardise** ✓   **c. thrifty**

3. Our English teacher insists that we do not use the adjective 'nice' because it is dull and _____.

   a. trite ✓   **b. delectable**   **c. administration**

4. After much discussion, Brian and Julie decided on a _____ location for their next holiday.

   a. interject   **b. definite** ✓   **c. jeopardise**

5. Jess polished off all the _____ cupcakes by herself!

   a. thrifty   **b. delectable** ✓   **c. trite**

6. Ben was _____ and waited until Wednesday to get half-price cinema tickets.

   a. hospitality   **b. thrifty** ✓   **c. stipulate**

7. Some parents were not happy with the _____ of the school, complaining that lessons started late and many teachers were absent.

   a. definite   **b. replete**   **c. administration** ✓

8. Please accept our _____ by coming to stay with us next year.

   a. delectable   **b. hospitality** ✓   **c. jeopardise**

9. Whilst it can be rude to _____, it often makes a debate more interesting.

   a. interject ✓   **b. thrifty**   **c. stipulate**

10. My email inbox is _____ with store promotions which do not interest me.

    a. trite   **b. definite**   **c. replete** ✓

Vocabulary 4

Learn the words below and then answer the questions that follow!

1. **Composed** (adj.): calm, serene, placid, controlled.
   Before giving her speech, Devika appeared to be cool and **composed**, yet her stomach was churning with nerves.

2. **Enmity** (n.): a state of active hostility or opposition; friction, tension.
   For centuries there was **enmity** and war between the Vikings and the people of the British Isles.

3. **Orthodox** (adj.): traditional, ordinary, normal.
   Jasdeep had a mysterious virus which could not be cured by **orthodox** medicine, so he turned to alternative treatments such as acupuncture.

4. **Consolidate** (v.): to strengthen, support; to combine, unite, merge.
   Years of work and training in the field **consolidated** Duncan's knowledge of biology.

5. **Tangible** (adj.): something that can be touched or felt; physical, real, perceptible.
   The tension in the room was almost **tangible** after the argument.

6. **Impede** (v.): to delay or prevent something; to hinder, to block.
   Failing to pay attention at school will **impede** a child's learning.

7. **Reduction** (n.): decrease, cutback, lowering, lessening.
   During the January sales, there were **reductions** offered throughout Westfield and shoppers could find real bargains.

8. **Satisfaction** (n.): fulfilment of wishes, contentment, pleasure.
   I felt great **satisfaction** when I passed my exams; at last all my hard work had paid off.

9. **Grandeur** (n.): splendour, magnificence, importance.
   You could sense the **grandeur** of the estate just from walking through its extensive gardens.

10. **Undefined** (adj.): unspecified, indeterminate, not clear.
    The faces in the painting were so **undefined** that it was difficult to work out who they were.

Exercise A: Synonyms

Write the word from the vocab list which is *most similar* in meaning next to each word listed below.

1. Hostility _____Enmity_____
2. Decrease _____Reduction_____
3. Splendour _____Grandeur_____
4. Traditional _____Othodox_____
5. Strengthen _____Consolidate_____
6. Real _____Tangible_____
7. Contentment _____Satisfaction_____
8. Unspecified _____Undefined_____
9. Calm _____Composed_____
10. Prevent _____Impede_____

VOCAB 4 WORD BANK

✓Composed ✓
✓ Enmity ✓
✓ Orthodox ✓
Consolidate ✓
✓Tangible ✓
✓Impede ✓
✓Reduction ✓
✓Satisfaction ✓
✓Grandeur ✓
✓Undefined ✓

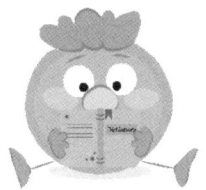

Exercise B: Complete the sentence

Write the most suitable word from the vocab list in the spaces below. You might need to change the form of the word; for instance, walk might become walked.

1. I felt an unexpected sense of _____satisfaction_____ once I had finished tidying my bedroom.

2. The trail of crumbs leading to Billy's bedroom was _____tangible_____ evidence that he had eaten the biscuits.

3. Alana's expression remained _____composed_____, meaning that no one realised how upset she was not to win the art prize.

4. Freddie did not stay out late as he knew lack of sleep would _____impede_____ his ability to study the next day.

5. In Shakespeare's play, there was great _____enmity_____ between Romeo's family, the Montagues, and Juliet's family, the Capulets.

6. A _____reduction_____ in the use of diesel cars will help to improve air quality in our cities.

7. The _____Grandeur_____ of London's museum buildings greatly impressed all the tourists.

8. Several small banks plan to _____consolidate_____ next year to form one large, single bank.

9. The rules of the game were _____undefined_____ so no-one knew exactly how to play.

10. Beatrice has a very _____Orthodox_____ taste in clothes and dislikes her sister's ripped jeans.

Exercise C: Complete the sentence

Select the most suitable word from the choices provided.

1. A fallen tree across the river _____d the flow of the water.

   a. undefined   **b. impede**   c. reduction

2. Joseph Stalin _____d his political power over many years before becoming leader of the Soviet Union.

   a. grandeur   b. tangible   **c. consolidate**

3. During the drama exam, while other pupils seemed flustered, Sam remained _____.

   a. orthodox   **b. composed**   c. enmity

4. Student _____ at school is at an all-time low after the headmaster left suddenly.

   a. impede   **b. satisfaction**   c. tangible

5. Oscar asked to see evidence of _____ benefits, such as a pay rise, before signing the new job contract.

   a. composed   **b. tangible**   c. grandeur

6. There was no _____ solution to Libby's problem so she had to come up with a more unusual plan.

   a. reduction   **b. orthodox**   c. consolidate

7. Dad lent my older sister his car for an _____ period of time, and did not say when he needed it back.

   a. composed   b. impede   **c. undefined**

8. The _____ of the Great Wall of China cannot be matched by any other structure.

   a. tangible   **b. grandeur**   **c. satisfaction**

9. There was a _____ in homelessness after charities received more funding.

   a. orthodox   **b. reduction**   c. impede

10. The _____ between cats and dogs is thousands of years old.

   a. enmity   b. composed   c. grandeur

Vocabulary 5

Learn the words below and then answer the questions that follow!

1. **Assailant** (n.): someone who attacks another person, attacker, mugger.
   The victim was unable to give many details about her **assailant** because the attack was over in seconds.

2. **Conspicuous** (adj.): clearly visible, obvious, noticeable.
   There was a **conspicuous** red stain on Leo's shirt that he could not hide from his mother.

3. **Cohesive** (adj.): stuck together, united, bonded.
   Alan, Temi and Abdul are a **cohesive** group of friends; they get on well and are always loyal to each other.

4. **Abhor** (v.): to hate, detest, loathe, disdain.
   I **abhor** the new school uniform because it is so drab and ugly.

5. **Deplete** (v.): to use up or drain supplies; diminish in quantity, reduce.
   When camping, your supplies of food and water can **deplete** rapidly if you are not careful with them.

6. **Frugal** (adj.): economical, tight or careful with money, sparing, thrifty.
   I had a **frugal** dinner consisting of plain rice and peas as I was saving money to pay for my holiday abroad.

7. **Prerequisite** (n.): a necessary prior condition for something to happen; essential requirement.
   A **prerequisite** of being a top sportsman is living a healthy lifestyle.

8. **Acrid** (adj.): unpleasantly bitter or pungent, acidic, sour.
   The factory billowed out **acrid** smoke while environmentalists protested at the gate.

9. **Shrewd** (adj.): having good judgement; clever, canny, intelligent.
   The **shrewd** investor made millions in just one year by buying and selling property.

10. **Daunting** (adj.): seeming difficult to deal with; intimidating, unnerving.
    The bungee jump was **daunting** but I knew I could do it if I remained calm.

Exercise A: Synonyms

Write the word from the vocab list which is *most similar* in meaning next to each word listed below.

1. Intelligent __shrewd__
2. Essential __prerequisite__
3. Obvious __conspicuous__
4. Reduce __deplete__
5. United __cohesive__
6. Intimidating __daunting__
7. Pungent __Acrid__
8. Loathe __Abhor__
9. Attacker __assailant__
10. Thrifty __Frugal__

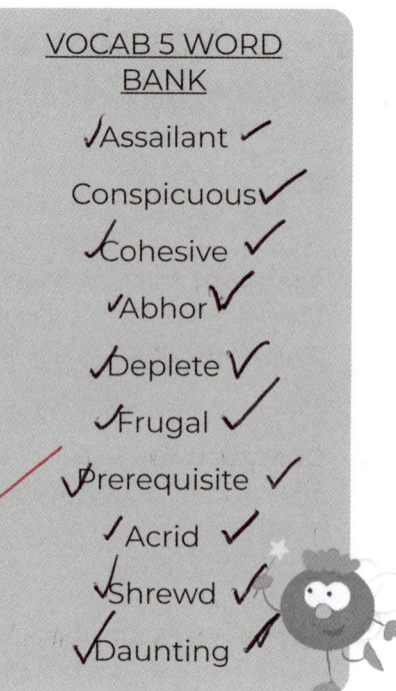

VOCAB 5 WORD BANK

✓Assailant ✓
Conspicuous ✓
✓Cohesive ✓
✓Abhor ✓
✓Deplete ✓
✓Frugal ✓
✓Prerequisite ✓
✓Acrid ✓
✓Shrewd ✓
✓Daunting ✓

Exercise B: Complete the sentence

Write the most suitable word from the vocab list in the spaces below. You might need to change the form of the word; for instance, walk might become walked.

1. I hoped that the __acrid__ smell would disappear, but it persisted for ages.

2. There are very few things that my mum __abhor__s, but one is bad language.

3. Police are doing everything in their power to catch the __assailant__.

4. My parents sat in the most __cohesive conspicuous.__ seats in the front row when I performed in the school musical.

5. A university degree is a __prerequisite__ for a career as a teacher.

6. At the start of the school year, our class went on an overnight trip to help us bond and become a more __cohesive__ unit.

7. The football manager made a few __shrewd__ changes to his team at half-time, and the players went on to win the game.

8. I need to be far more __frugal__ after overspending last month.

9. Many natural resources will __deplete__ in the next 50 years due to climate change.

10. Confronting bullies can be a __daunting__ task but it can stop them picking on you.

Exercise C: Complete the sentence

Select the most suitable word from the choices provided.

1. Louise was _____ and hated spending any money if she could avoid it.

    a. deplete   **b. cohesive**   **c. frugal**

2. The child faced the _____ prospect of three exams in one day.

    a. acrid   **b. assailant**   **c. daunting**

3. Dad made the _____ move of buying a car just before prices went up.

    a. shrewd   **b. abhor**   **c. conspicuous**

4. A _____ of entering some foreign countries is obtaining a visa.

    a. assailant   **b. frugal**   **c. prerequisite**

5. My sister _____s waste and always tries to recycle as much as possible.

    a. abhor   **b. cohesive**   **c. conspicuous**

6. Even when I held my nose, the _____ odour of smoke overwhelmed me.

    a. daunting   **b. acrid**   **c. shrewd**

7. Liz wore an array of shiny and _____ jewellery to the fashion show.

    a. deplete   **b. abhor**   **c. conspicuous**

8. The _____ fled the scene in a black BMW and the police are now looking for witnesses.

    a. assailant   **b. abhor**   **c. prerequisite**

9. The rugby team is not a _____ group since the players do not yet know each other well.

    a. frugal   **b. cohesive**   **c. daunting**

10. The population of polar bears has _____d over the last 10 years despite our best conservation efforts.

    a. deplete   **b. acrid**   **c. shrewd**

Vocabulary 6

Learn the words below and then answer the questions that follow!

1. **Preposterous** (adj.): laughable, utterly absurd, ridiculous.
   The ship's captain made the **preposterous** suggestion of sailing in the stormy conditions.

2. **Gratuitous** (adj.): done without good reason; excessive, uncalled for.
   Many parents have accused modern video games of showing **gratuitous** violence.

3. **Verification** (n.): proof, confirmation, validation.
   Darcy needs **verification** that he attended school in England for his Australian visa.

4. **Hindrance** (n.): obstacle, barrier, restriction.
   Too many people with differing opinions working on the project will be a **hindrance**, not a benefit.

5. **Almanac** (n.): an annual calendar with important dates and information.
   The school **almanac** outlines all the important dates during each term.

6. **Dilapidated** (adj.): in a state of ruin, neglected, run down.
   What was once a wealthy area is now **dilapidated** and poverty-stricken following the economic crisis.

7. **Raucous** (adj.): unpleasantly loud, harsh, rowdy, unruly.
   You could hear the **raucous** chanting from the football stadium from miles away.

8. **Resonate** (v.): to produce a vibrating sound or echo, reverberate; to evoke, have an effect on.
   Music from the bar **resonated** throughout the whole neighbourhood.

9. **Empathy** (n.): ability to understand and share the feelings and emotions of another person; sensitivity, compassion.
   Emmy is characterised by her **empathy**; she is always there for her friends to confide in.

10. **Predicament** (n.): a difficult or awkward situation, muddle, dilemma.
    Saffy was in a **predicament** when she could not find her homework and the lesson was about to begin.

Exercise A: Synonyms

Write the word from the vocab list which is *most similar* in meaning next to each word listed below.

1. Proof _____verification_____
2. Neglected _____dilapidated_____
3. Obstacle _____Hindrance_____
4. Sensitivity _____empathy_____
5. Dilemma _____predicament_____
6. Excessive _____Gratuitous_____
7. Harsh _____raucous_____
8. Evoke _____resonate_____
9. Calendar _____almanac_____
10. Ridiculous _____preposterous_____

Exercise B: Complete the sentence

Write the most suitable word from the vocab list in the spaces below. You might need to change the form of the word; for instance, walk might become walked.

1. The novel _____resonate_____d with me as it reminded me of my happy childhood.

2. Maybe if you had a bit more _____empathy_____, you would understand how Marty was feeling.

3. Nick needs _____verification_____ of his age before he is allowed into the music festival.

4. Mum said I could not watch the movie as it contained too much _____raucous_____ gratu bad language.

5. Tom put me in a real _____predicament_____ after he told me Jemima's secrets!

6. My sister said I was more of a _____Hindrance_____ than a help in the kitchen when she was preparing lunch.

7. The theatre audience was rowdy and _____gratuitou_____ so the actors struggled to continue.

8. Trying to climb between two hotel balconies on the 26th floor is a _____preposterous_____ idea.

9. The _____dilapidated_____ old ship had browned with rust in the harbour.

10. A nautical _____almanac_____ gives information about the tides and stars to help sailors navigate their ships.

Exercise C: Complete the sentence

Select the most suitable word from the choices provided.

1. The lawyer demanded _____ of the witnesses' statements during the trial.

    a. empathy   **b. resonate**   **c. verification**

2. Helena thought the tutor's harsh criticism of her presentation was _____

    a. raucous   **b. gratuitous**   **c. almanac**

3. My aunt has decided she wants to renovate the _____ old shed in her garden.

    a. dilapidated   **b. hindrance**   **c. preposterous**

4. Rowley faced a difficult _____, since by mistake he had accepted two party invitations for the same evening.

    a. resonate   **b. raucous**   **c. predicament**

5. My dad's company sends out a yearly _____ detailing key events and dates.

    a. gratuitous   **b. almanac**   **c. hindrance**

6. A _____ group of teenagers hanging out on our street woke everyone up during the night.

    a. resonate   **b. raucous**   **c. dilapidated**

7. Daniel's belief in aliens and ghosts is simply _____ as he is a trained scientist!

    a. empathy   **b. gratuitous**   **c. preposterous**

8. The ambulance's siren _____d through the streets of London.

    a. resonate   **b. raucous**   **c. verification**

9. Psychologists believe that showing _____ for others is a sign of a balanced and healthy mind.

    a. almanac   **b. empathy**   **c. predicament**

10. Mobile phones can be a _____ to sleep, because the blue light they emit stimulates our eyes and brain.

    a. gratuitous   **b. dilapidated**   **c. hindrance**

Vocabulary 7

Learn the words below and then answer the questions that follow!

1. **Torrid** (adj.): very hot and dry, sweltering, scorching; intense or difficult (emotions).
   The **torrid** temperatures have caused the farmer's crops to wilt and die.

2. **Abdomen** (n.): stomach, gut, intestines, middle, belly.
   I had food poisoning after eating contaminated oysters, which caused intense pain in my **abdomen**.

3. **Repugnant** (adj.): repulsive, disgusting, foul, vile.
   Mum discovered that the **repugnant** smell in my brother's room was coming from rotting food left under his bed.

4. **Dehydrated** (adj.) dried up, thirsty, parched, having had moisture removed.
   Travellers in the desert must drink vast amounts of water to avoid becoming **dehydrated** in the hot sun.

5. **Sanction** (n.): a punishment, penalty, deterrent.
   In 1963, the United States imposed economic **sanctions** on Cuba, to limit certain types of trade.

6. **Tedious** (adj.): tiresome, dull, unexciting, boring.
   It's **tedious** to have to always clear up after my younger siblings.

7. **Admonish** (v.): to reprimand, scold, tell off.
   Karen had to **admonish** her daughter for telling lies about where she had been.

8. **Exude** (v.): to produce, emit, give off (e.g. a smell); to show a quality or feeling.
   In social situations, Max **exudes** confidence and charms everyone.

9. **Invoke** (v.): to use something/someone to support your argument, call on, summon.
   I **invoked** Darwin and his theory of evolution during the debate about extinction.

10. **Augment** (v.): to increase, add to something, enlarge.
    If the government **augments** the NHS spending budget then there will be more money available to improve hospitals.

Exercise A: Synonyms

Write the word from the vocab list which is *most similar* in meaning next to each word listed below.

1. Parched _____dehydrated_____
2. Punishment _____sanction_____
3. Increase _____augment_____
4. Stomach _____abdomen_____
5. Boring _____tedious_____
6. Reprimand _____admonish_____
7. Scorching _____torrid_____
8. Emit _____exude_____
9. Summon _____invoke_____
10. Disgusting _____repugnant_____

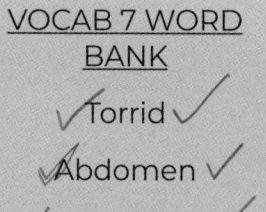

VOCAB 7 WORD BANK
- Torrid
- Abdomen
- Repugnant
- Dehydrated
- Sanction
- Tedious
- Admonish
- Exude
- Invoke
- Augment

Exercise B: Complete the sentence

Write the most suitable word from the vocab list in the spaces below. You might need to change the form of the word; for instance, walk might become walked.

1. Today, technology is used regularly in the classroom to _____augment_____ children's learning.

2. Abdullah feared that the teacher would _____sanction / admonish_____ him for not finishing his project.

3. My brother refused to wash the dishes as he said it was a _____tedious_____ task.

4. Theo has been doing sit-ups recently to strengthen his _____abdomen_____ and core.

5. Jo did not _____exude_____ any other novelists in his essay so he did not achieve full marks.

6. The new teacher _____invoke_____d calm and authority, commanding everyone's attention.

7. Norm had not washed for four days and he smelled truly _____repugnant_____.

8. I always carry water with me during a race so that I do not become _____dehydrated_____.

9. At school, the _____sanction_____ for not handing in homework is a lunchtime detention.

10. My cousin loved his holiday in northern Australia, despite the harsh climate and _____torrid_____ heat.

Exercise C: Complete the sentence

Select the most suitable word from the choices provided.

1. The diffuser in our living room _____s a powerful scent of lavender.
    a: augment   b: dehydrated   c: exude

2. Mark's memory was so good that he could always _____ numerous statistics in his arguments.
    a: abdomen   b: invoke   c: repugnant

3. Jonathan tore two muscles in his _____ in a water-skiing accident.
    a: tedious   b: sanction   c: abdomen

4. After several years as a vegetarian, Minnie found the idea of eating meat completely _____.
    a: repugnant   b: dehydrated   c: torrid

5. I always found the car journey to Grandma's in Wales very long and _____
    a: tedious   b: sanction   c: admonish

6. I was sweating all through the _____ heat of the afternoon.
    a: dehydrated   b: exude   c: torrid

7. Jack had to _____ his dog, Muffin, for causing a mess in the house.
    a: admonish   b: augment   c: abdomen

8. Leila decided to _____ her pocket money by finding well-paid work as a babysitter.
    a: sanction   b: augment   c: admonish

9. Countries which refused to stop the killing of whales were faced with tough trade _____s.
    a. tedious   b: torrid   c: sanction

10. After having the winter vomiting bug, Mariam felt tired and _____
    a. dehydrated   b. abdomen   c: invoke

Vocabulary 8

Learn the words below and then answer the questions that follow!

1. **Dissuade** (v.): to persuade someone not to do something, discourage, prevent.
   I tried to **dissuade** James from playing football in the classroom in case he broke a window.

2. **Mediocre** (adj.): average or poor quality, ordinary.
   In the town's art show, a few of the paintings were highly impressive, most were **mediocre** and the odd one truly dreadful.

3. **Brandish** (v.): to wave or flourish as a threat, wield, hold in the air.
   The gunman **brandished** a weapon and ordered people to get down on the floor.

4. **Rabid** (adj.): extreme, fanatical, over-enthusiastic, passionate; an animal infected with rabies.
   The football supporters' club consisted of a small yet **rabid** fanbase, who went to every single game.

5. **Pacify** (v.): to calm anger or agitation or excitement, bring peace, quieten.
   The government tried to **pacify** the angry protesters before somebody was hurt.

6. **Bountiful** (adj.): great in number, lavish, abundant, plentiful.
   The ocean provides us with a **bountiful** supply of fresh fish.

7. **Undeniable** (adj.): beyond question, true, indisputable.
   It was **undeniable** that Jim was the best in the class at English because he always received top marks.

8. **Linguist** (n.): a person skilled in speaking foreign languages; a person who studies language; interpreter, translator.
   Tom is a gifted **linguist** and can speak four languages fluently.

9. **Recur** (v.): to occur repeatedly, happen again, be repeated.
   Many of us experience dreams in childhood which then **recur** throughout our lives.

10. **Deplore** (v.): to feel or express strong disapproval, be shocked by, abhor.
    I **deplore** anyone who refuses to donate food to the food bank as they must be very selfish.

Exercise A: Synonyms

Write the word from the vocab list which is *most similar* in meaning next to each word listed below.

1. Translator _linguist_____

2. Quieten _____

3. Average _____

4. Repeat _____

5. Plentiful _____

6. Extreme _____

7. Disapprove _____

8. Wield _____

9. Discourage _____

10. Indisputable_____

Exercise B: Complete the sentence

Write the most suitable word from the vocab list in the spaces below. You might need to change the form of the word; for instance, walk might become walked.

1. The referee _____ed a yellow card at the player who had committed a foul.

2. My mum's favourite restaurant serves only _____ food, but she adores the staff.

3. I tried to _____ my friends from voting against the plan to make our school canteen vegetarian-only.

4. The Swiss ambassador hired a _____ to assist him on his business trip to China.

5. The corn harvest was _____ last year, because the weather conditions were perfect.

6. Martin managed to _____ his tearful little sister by lending her his iPad.

7. Ginny's bruises were _____ evidence that she had been fighting in the playground again.

8. The doctor told Ted that his stomach bug might _____ if he ate too much rich food.

9. Tom was frightened when a drooling, _____ dog approached his car.

10. My mother _____s the moths that eat away at her fine wool jumpers.

Exercise C: Complete the sentence

Select the most suitable word from the choices provided.

1. My brother will study French and Spanish at university; he is a keen _____.

   a. brandish   **b. dissuade**   **c. linguist**

2. Most parents _____ excessive screen time for children as it is known to be bad for them.

   a. undeniable   **b. deplore**   **c. recur**

3. The new treaty was intended to _____ the aggressive hostile forces.

   a. pacify   **b. rabid**   **c. bountiful**

4. Although I thought the film was outstanding, it only received _____ reviews.

   a. dissuade   **b. mediocre**   **c. deplore**

5. Almost all scientists agree that climate change is _____ and we must act now to prevent it.

   a. linguist   **b. pacify**   **c. undeniable**

6. The police arrested the _____ group of protesters for being too aggressive.

   a. mediocre   **b. rabid**   **c. recur**

7. Geeta tried to _____ Tim from making a chess move that would cause him to lose the game.

   a. dissuade   **b. bountiful**   **c. deplore**

8. Thoughts about my future always _____ when I'm lying in bed at night trying to fall asleep.

   a. pacify   **b. recur**   **c. linguist**

9. Police apprehended the man who _____ed a knife at the Tube station.

   a. mediocre   **b. dissuade**   **c. brandish**

10. The tropical island has a _____ supply of fresh water from lakes and streams.

    a. bountiful   **b. rabid**   **c. recur**

Vocabulary 9

Learn the words below and then answer the questions that follow!

1. **Parity** (n.): being equal, similarity, uniformity, equivalence.
   We need to achieve **parity** of incomes between male and female employees.

2. **Wield** (v.): to hold, brandish, exert, display.
   The corrupt politician managed to **wield** enormous power over the prime minister.

3. **Ebony** (adj.) jet-black, very dark in colour; made of black ebony wood.
   Snow White is often depicted with pale skin to contrast with her **ebony**-black hair.

4. **Tsunami** (n.): a tidal wave, a huge wave caused by an event such as an earthquake.
   A **tsunami** can have a devastating effect on coastal towns, destroying entire communities in minutes.

5. **Stupendous** (adj.): astonishing, remarkable, amazing.
   Critics agreed that the highly regarded production of Macbeth at the National Theatre was **stupendous**.

6. **Suave** (adj.): smooth, polished, impeccable, sophisticated.
   The bridegroom looked **suave** in his suit, compared with his usual scruffy appearance.

7. **Scrutiny** (n.): critical examination, close analysis, inspection.
   The prince came under great **scrutiny** from journalists over the financial scandal he was involved in.

8. **Canon** (n.): a law or rule (often decreed by a church); standard, regulation.
   The unfair election went against the **canon** of equal rights for all.

9. **Transfusion** (n.): the transfer of blood or other fluids into a human or animal; transfer of ideas.
   The victim of a motorbike accident required a blood **transfusion** as part of her treatment.

10. **Eulogy** (n.): a speech praising someone (often at funerals); tribute, dedication.
    Family members usually prepare a **eulogy** for the funeral of a relative to highlight their achievements.

Exercise A: Synonyms

Write the word from the vocab list which is *most similar* in meaning next to each word listed below.

	VOCAB 9 WORD BANK
	Parity
	Wield
	Ebony
	Tsunami
	Stupendous
	Suave
	Scrutiny
	Canon
	Transfusion
	Eulogy

1. Regulation _____

2. Equivalence_____

3. Transfer _____

4. Amazing _____

5. Sophisticated_____

6. Tidal wave _____

7. Black _____

8. Brandish _____

9. Inspection _____

10. Tribute _____

Exercise B: Complete the sentence

Write the most suitable word from the vocab list in the spaces below. You might need to change the form of the word; for instance, walk might become walked.

1. Queen Elizabeth II read a moving _____ at her mother's funeral.

2. The knight _____ed his sword with a skill that had never been seen before.

3. It is said that many animals run to high ground well before a _____ occurs.

4. James Bond is known for being a super-cool and _____ secret agent.

5. The Spanish villa boasts _____ views of the ocean.

6. Many people give blood in order to save the lives of those who need a _____.

7. Some religious beliefs may contradict the _____ of scientific reason.

8. Sam was put off applying to drama school due to the constant public _____ actors endure.

9. Panthers are best identified by their sleek, _____ coats.

10. At school, the sports coaches demanded pay _____ with the music teachers.

Exercise C: Complete the sentence

Select the most suitable word from the choices provided.

1. The massive _____ was caused by earth tremors off the coast of Indonesia.

    a: tsunami　　　　**b: canon**　　　　**c: transfusion**

2. Napoleon could no longer _____ power over all of Europe after his defeat in Russia.

    a: canon　　　　**b: wield**　　　　**c: eulogy**

3. Mark spent a _____ amount of money on food and drink during his holiday.

    a: suave　　　　**b: ebony**　　　　**c: stupendous**

4. The patient with severe food poisoning had a _____ of fluids via a drip.

    a: eulogy　　　　**b: parity**　　　　**c: transfusion**

5. Many people believe that the Biblical _____ offers us the truth about life.

    a: ebony　　　　**b: stupendous**　　　　**c: canon**

6. Ismail looked _____ in his new suit but did you see its eye-watering price tag?

    a: suave　　　　**b: scrutiny**　　　　**c: tsunami**

7. There was an assortment of beautiful _____ carvings in the bazaar.

    a: ebony　　　　**b: stupendous**　　　　**c: parity**

8. Seamus Heaney wrote many moving poems as a _____ for his late mother.

    a: canon　　　　**b: eulogy**　　　　**c: ebony**

9. Mary and Lola's _____ on the tennis court is well known, therefore it is hard to predict who will win the match.

    a: scrutiny　　　　**b: wield**　　　　**c: parity**

10. Politicians and business-owners face _____ by lawyers to ensure that their behaviour is honest.

    a: transfusion　　　　**b: suave**　　　　**c: scrutiny**

Vocabulary 10

Learn the words below and then answer the questions that follow!

1. **Thesis** (n.): a theory, line of argument; extended essay written by university students as part of their degree.
   Mary is midway through writing her **thesis** on the development of butterflies.

2. **Accountable** (adj.): held responsible, expected to explain or justify something, liable.
   The Prime Minister must be held **accountable** for the failing government.

3. **Diabolical** (adj.): like the evil of the devil; dreadful, extremely unpleasant.
   The driving examiner refused to pass Freddie after his **diabolical** attempt at parking almost caused an accident.

4. **Vandalism** (n.): the act of defacing or damaging someone's property; destruction, harm.
   Police officers need to do more to combat **vandalism** in our neighbourhood.

5. **Atrocities** (n.pl.): act of brutality or cruelty (often violent), injustice, abuse.
   The goblins committed numerous **atrocities** during the war against the elves.

6. **Subterranean** (adj.): existing under the surface of the earth, buried, underground.
   In the UK, moles are the most common **subterranean** mammal; they often burrow under gardens.

7. **Plagiarise** (v.): to copy someone's work and claim it as your own, steal.
   If you **plagiarise** other people's homework, you will face serious consequences.

8. **Centenary** (n.): the hundredth anniversary of a significant event, a hundredth year commemoration.
   In 2018, events were held to mark the **centenary** of the end of World War I.

9. **Tutelage** (n.): protection or authority over something, guidance, guardianship.
   University students are under the **tutelage** of a supervisor, who will advise them.

10. **Ultimatum** (n.): final demand or order, threat before something bad occurs.
    The school gave Fiona an **ultimatum**: either improve her behaviour or face expulsion.

Exercise A: Synonyms

Write the word from the vocab list which is *most similar* in meaning next to each word listed below.

1. Copy   _____
2. Underground_____
3. Devilish   _____
4. Anniversary_____
5. Responsible_____
6. Guidance   _____
7. Essay   _____
8. Order   _____
9. Damage   _____
10. Abuses   _____

VOCAB 10 WORD BANK

Thesis

Accountable

Diabolical

Vandalism

Atrocities

Subterranean

Plagiarise

Centenary

Tutelage

Ultimatum

Exercise B: Complete the sentence

Write the most suitable word from the vocab list in the spaces below. You might need to change the form of the word; for instance, walk might become walked.

1. Queen Elizabeth II attended a service for the _____ of the Battle of the Somme.

2. Jamie was held _____ for losing the football because he was the eldest sibling, although Suki had kicked it over the fence.

3. The UN condemned the _____ committed by the terrorist group.

4. Lily was caught trying to _____ her friend's work during the test.

5. Banksy's art has been described as a thought-provoking form of _____.

6. Professor Singh was inspirational to the students under his _____.

7. Mum gave Ali an _____: either sit still at the table or go upstairs and miss lunch.

8. Under the castle there was a _____ network of secret rooms and passages.

9. Darwin's _____ on evolution was one of the most important breakthroughs in biology.

10. Conditions in prisons in Roman times were said to be inhumane and _____.

Exercise C: Complete the sentence

Select the most suitable word from the choices provided.

1. The Arsenal player gave his club an _____, saying that if they did not increase his salary he would transfer to West Ham.

   a. plagiarise   **b. ultimatum**   **c. accountable**

2. Amy loved the colourful patterns of graffiti art but her mum said it was _____.

   a. atrocities   **b. thesis**   **c. vandalism**

3. The composer was fined in court for having _____d another artist's song.

   a. plagiarise   **b. centenary**   **c. accountable**

4. Norman was looking for inspiration for the title of his university _____.

   a. diabolical   **b. tutelage**   **c. thesis**

5. Plants gain all their nutrients through _____ roots.

   a. ultimatum   **b. vandalism**   **c. subterranean**

6. Without Aunt Victoria's _____, I wouldn't have passed all my exams.

   a. centenary   **b. thesis**   **c. tutelage**

7. Dom had a _____ voice but insisted on hurting our ears with his singing!

   a. diabolical   **b. plagiarise**   **c. accountable**

8. By learning from horrific war _____ of the past, we can ensure they never happen again in the future.

   a. atrocities   **b. vandalism**   **c. ultimatum**

9. If I reach the _____ of my birth, I will certainly have lived a long life!

   a. tutelage   **b. centenary**   **c. subterranean**

10. Jane heroically announced she was the person _____ for our failed experiment, after none of us came forward.

    a. tutelage   **b. atrocities**   **c. accountable**

Vocabulary 11

Learn the words below and then answer the questions that follow!

1. **Vaccine** (n.): a medicine that produces immunity against a disease; inoculation.
   Babies receive the tetanus **vaccine** to prevent them from catching the disease.

2. **Testify** (v.): to give evidence (often in a court of law), bear witness.
   I can **testify** that James came to work on time today as I saw him arrive.

3. **Compensate** (v.): to pay back, reimburse, reward; to reduce, counteract.
   The employee felt that his salary increase did not **compensate** for the extremely long hours he had to work.

4. **Rhapsody** (n.): elation, joy, delight; a piece of music with no formal structure, melody, arrangement.
   The orchestra began the concert with a lively **rhapsody**.

5. **Temperamental** (adj.): having changes in mood, volatile, overemotional.
   Jonny is so **temperamental**: one minute he's happy and the next he's depressed.

6. **Volition** (n.): free will, choice, voluntary act.
   Maggie made the decision to move abroad of her own **volition**, and was not influenced in any way.

7. **Lucid** (adj.): clear, easily understood, rational, logical; bright or luminous.
   Zach gave a **lucid** account of his skiing accident, remembering every detail.

8. **Telepathy** (n.): the ability to communicate through the power of the mind; mind-reading, intuition.
   Malia and I seem to communicate using **telepathy**, because we sense each other's thoughts.

9. **Transcend** (v.): to go beyond the limits of something, surpass, exceed.
   No writer will ever **transcend** the achievements of William Shakespeare, who is the most famous author in English history.

10. **Susceptible** (adj.): receptive to, vulnerable to, open to; inclined or likely to.
    My grandad is **susceptible** to internet scams because he is so trusting.

Exercise A: Synonyms

Write the word from the vocab list which is *most similar* in meaning next to each word listed below.

1. Counteract _____
2. Inoculation _____
3. Mind-reading _____
4. Melody _____
5. Clear _____
6. Surpass _____
7. Witness _____
8. Choice _____
9. Vulnerable _____
10. Volatile _____

Exercise B: Complete the sentence

Write the most suitable word from the vocab list in the spaces below. You might need to change the form of the word; for instance, walk might become walked.

1. The book was beautifully written, with its precise and _____ prose.

2. My dog seems to communicate with me via _____, as he can sense my moods.

3. Olly cannot swim and without his life-jacket he would be _____ to drowning.

4. Damian chose fruit rather than ice-cream not of his own _____, but because his grandmother made him.

5. The Jedi warrior learned to _____ death and become a spiritual being.

6. I had several _____s against tropical diseases before I went travelling abroad.

7. One of Queen's most famous songs is the musical masterpiece Bohemian _____.

8. Since there was no witness to _____ against him in court, the burglar went free.

9. Nothing can _____ for the photos I lost when my phone was stolen.

10. My cat is so _____ because first she hisses at me and then she snuggles on my lap.

Exercise C: Complete the sentence

Select the most suitable word from the choices provided.

1.   Bobby left the party early of his own _____, not because anyone told him to.

     a. rhapsody   **b. volition**   **c. temperamental**

2.   What we learn at school _____s the traditional subjects, because we are also taught important values.

     a. transcend   **b. susceptible**   **c. testify**

3.   Granny's old car is a bit _____; it often won't start in cold weather.

     a. lucid   **b. rhapsody**   **c. temperamental**

4.   Anya's _____ description of the mountains made me feel as though I was there!

     a. telepathy   **b. lucid**   **c. compensate**

5.   One day we will have a _____ to prevent many types of cancer.

     a. vaccine   **b. rhapsody**   **c. transcend**

6.   Michael has a weak immune system and is _____ to all types of illnesses.

     a. telepathy   **b. volition**   **c. susceptible**

7.   Some people, such as psychics, believe in _____, however it cannot be scientifically proven.

     a. vaccine   **b. telepathy**   **c. transcend**

8.   Aunt Betsy went into a _____ over the delicious cake at the tearoom.

     a. lucid   **b. rhapsody**   **c. temperamental**

9.   My left eye is weak, so my right eye must work harder to _____

     a. rhapsody   **b. telepathy**   **c. compensate**

10.   The fingerprint expert was called to _____ at the murder trial.

     a. testify   **b. transcend**   **c. susceptible**

Vocabulary 12

Learn the words below and then answer the questions that follow!

1. **Tyrannical** (adj.): exercising power cruelly; controlling, oppressive.
The **tyrannical** headmaster ignored our protests and banned us from playing football during break time.

2. **Conceited** (adj.): excessively proud, vain, self-obsessed.
Harry is so **conceited** that he loves staring at his reflection in the mirror.

3. **Fluctuate** (v.): to rise and fall, vary, alternate, change.
The travel company's profits **fluctuate** enormously between summer and winter.

4. **Armoury** (n.): a place where weapons are kept; depot, arsenal.
The law states that guns must be kept in an **armoury** so that only those authorised can access them.

5. **Impervious** (adj.): unaffected by, invulnerable to; waterproof, impenetrable.
Marcus kept working outside in the hot sun, seemingly **impervious** to the heat.

6. **Upheaval** (n.): disruption, upset, major change, overhaul.
Moving from the countryside to the city was a major **upheaval** for Mishka's family.

7. **Catalyst** (n.): a substance that accelerates a reaction; a person or thing that facilitates an event, impetus, stimulus.
The student riots were seen as a **catalyst** for change within the university system.

8. **Sinew** (n.): a cord that connects muscle to bone (similar to a tendon); fibre, strength.
Brian had the body of an elite athlete, with every muscle and **sinew** trained to perfection.

9. **Rebuke** (v.): to reprimand, scold, tell off.
My piano teacher **rebuked** me when it was clear that I had not practised my scales.

10. **Abundant** (adj.): plentiful, large in quantity, rich, bountiful.
In the summer, our garden is **abundant** with scented flowers planted in every flowerbed.

Exercise A: Synonyms

Write the word from the vocab list which is *most similar* in meaning next to each word listed below.

Tyrannical

Conceited

Fluctuate

Armoury

Impervious

Upheaval

Catalyst

Sinew

Rebuke

Abundant

1. Vain _____

2. Stimulus _____

3. Unaffected _____

4. Reprimand _____

5. Arsenal _____

6. Plentiful _____

7. Fibre _____

8. Disruption _____

9. Vary _____

10. Oppressive _____

Exercise B: Complete the sentence

Write the most suitable word from the vocab list in the spaces below. You might need to change the form of the word; for instance, walk might become walked.

1. Naomi never had to _____ her students because they were always well behaved.

2. Our team's performance _____d last year; we started the season well but then lost every game.

3. Everyone prefers a kind, brave leader instead of someone _____ and mean.

4. Before the paintball match, we had to choose our guns from the _____.

5. Lisa picked up the heavy shopping bags with ease, _____ to their weight.

6. Failing my mock exams acted as a _____ for my change in attitude because after that I was determined to do better.

7. The _____ marine life in coral reefs is disappearing due to global warming.

8. Problems with the new computer system caused a major _____ at Dad's company.

9. The traditional moccasin shoe worn by Native Americans was made of soft leather

    sewn together with animal _____.

10. It is very _____ of you to always think your work is the best in the class.

Exercise C: Complete the sentence

Select the most suitable word from the choices provided.

1. The Tube strikes in London caused a major _____ for commuters.

   a. fluctuate   b. conceited   c. upheaval

2. The Scottish king had many kinds of guns and other weapons in his _____

   a. armoury   b. tyrannical   c. impervious

3. Mum had to _____ Louis for his lack of manners when he started eating with his mouth open.

   a. catalyst   b. rebuke   c. sinew

4. There's often little difference between acting confidently and seeming _____

   a. abundant   b. conceited   c. upheaval

5. Dominic was _____ in his role as team captain; he shouted at everyone rather than encouraging them.

   a. tyrannical   b. sinew   c. armoury

6. The chemical reaction will take hours unless we use a _____ such as calcium carbonate to speed things up.

   a. rebuke   b. fluctuate   c. catalyst

7. Tropical rainforests contain the most _____ variety of animal and plant-life to be found anywhere.

   a. abundant   b. impervious   c. rebuke

8. Celia strained every _____ trying to push the car out of the mud.

   a. conceited   b. tyrannical   c. sinew

9. Darren had remained slim for the last few years, unlike Mandev, whose weight seemed to _____.

   a. upheaval   b. fluctuate   c. abundant

10. My wellington boots are completely _____ to water, so my feet stay dry.

    a. catalyst   b. impervious   c. rebuke

Vocabulary 13

Learn the words below and then answer the questions that follow!

1. **Tact** (n.): sensitivity, understanding, diplomacy, discretion.
   The police inspector broke the bad news to me with **tact** and sensitivity.

2. **Ostracise** (v.): to exclude (from a social group), shun, snub.
   Fred felt **ostracised** by the team when, after missing the penalty, he was ignored in the changing room.

3. **Vigilant** (adj.): watchful of possible danger, observant, on the lookout.
   When walking home alone late at night, I must be **vigilant** and aware of danger.

4. **Dismissive** (adj.): indifferent or uncaring, scornful, contemptuous.
   Mum was **dismissive** of my plans to build a tree house in the garden because she knew I would never get around to it.

5. **Tolerance** (n.): endurance of, acceptance, open-mindedness.
   Clara's **tolerance** of Tom's silly singing is admirable; we don't know how she puts up with him.

6. **Transfer** (n.): move, shift, relocation, transplant.
   The EU is likely to approve a **transfer** of wealth from richer to poorer nations.

7. **Risible** (adj.): ridiculous, absurd, comical.
   The film's cheap special effects were **risible**; anyone could see that the ghosts were puppets.

8. **Inherent** (adj.): ingrained, innate, natural, built-in.
   Dogs, being loyal creatures, have the **inherent** desire to protect their owners.

9. **Advocacy** (n.): support for, backing for, calling for, pushing for.
   Martin Luther King is known for his **advocacy** of civil rights; he spoke out against racial inequality.

10. **Adjourn** (v.): to pause, break off, finish (e.g. a meeting, legal case, or a game) with the intention of resuming later.
    We had to **adjourn** the meeting for a lunch break but agreed to resume at 2pm.

Exercise A: Synonyms

Write the word from the vocab list which is *most similar* in meaning next to each word listed below.

1. Innate _____

2. Acceptance _____

3. Support _____

4. Scornful _____

5. Observant _____

6. Exclude _____

7. Shift _____

8. Discretion _____

9. Pause _____

10. Absurd _____

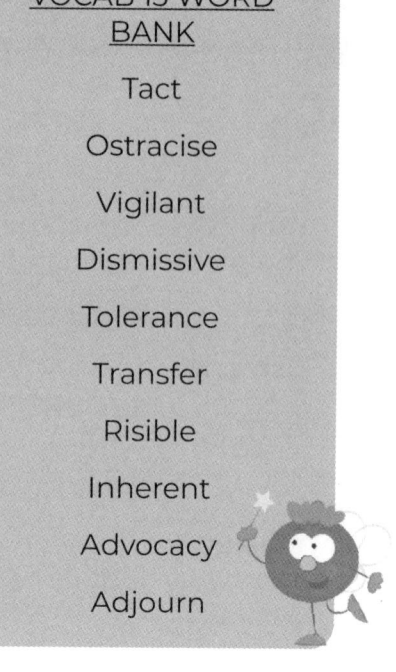

VOCAB 13 WORD BANK

Tact

Ostracise

Vigilant

Dismissive

Tolerance

Transfer

Risible

Inherent

Advocacy

Adjourn

Exercise B: Complete the sentence

Write the most suitable word from the vocab list in the spaces below. You might need to change the form of the word; for instance, walk might become walked.

1. The star player handed in a _____ request because he said he would earn more money at another club.

2. I was _____ of my friend's holiday plan as I knew she could not afford it.

3. The judge decided to _____ the case until the next day.

4. The politician was well known for his _____ of cheaper university fees.

5. There are _____ risks when launching rockets into Space.

6. Magda said it would be unkind to _____ and ignore Dilan just because his older brother had been expelled from school.

7. The idea that Larry will learn to play the flute is _____ because there is no way he will practise enough.

8. It is important that we express _____ towards all cultures and nationalities.

9. You need to be _____ on the Tube as sometimes pickpockets steal phones.

10. The shopkeeper showed _____ in dealing with difficult customers.

Exercise C: Complete the sentence

Select the most suitable word from the choices provided.

1. The murder trial was _____ed because the jury had requested further information.

    a. tolerance   **b. adjourn**   **c. inherent**

2. The night watchman must remain _____ in case intruders appear at the gate.

    a. vigilant   **b. ostracise**   **c. advocacy**

3. Ed is always so rude and _____ if people are critical of his work.

    a. tact   **b. transfer**   **c. dismissive**

4. Alex's idea to climb Mount Everest in a day was clearly _____

    a. risible   **b. adjourn**   **c. vigilant**

5. There are _____ dangers in extreme sports, but that's what makes them so exciting!

    a. ostracise   **b. transfer**   **c. inherent**

6. Try to be understanding and allow some _____ for opposing views.

    a. dismissive   **b. risible**   **c. tolerance**

7. Whilst I wouldn't publicise my _____ of the new law, I believe it is a good idea.

    a. advocacy   **b. vigilant**   **c. dismissive**

8. Could you please do a bank _____ for the money you owe me from dinner yesterday?

    a. adjourn   **b. transfer**   **c. tolerance**

9. If Norma had a little more _____, she could have easily avoided upsetting Sue.

    a. dismissive   **b. inherent**   **c. tact**

10. The old lady was declared a witch and _____d by the other medieval villagers.

    a. ostracise   **b. transfer**   **c. vigilant**

Vocabulary 14

Learn the words below and then answer the questions that follow!

1. **Officiate** (v.): to be in charge of, manage, referee, supervise.
   Only very experienced referees can **officiate** at Premier League football matches.

2. **Albino** (adj.): condition that causes an absence of skin colour; pale white.
   Albino rats have white skin and red eyes.

3. **Philanthropy** (n.): the act of helping the poor and less fortunate, charity, compassion.
   Everyone should try to engage in **philanthropy** and donate money to charities.

4. **Fanatic** (n.): a person with an obsessive interest in something, extremist, zealot.
   Jasmine is a tennis **fanatic** and watches the sport obsessively, both on TV and at live events.

5. **Resplendent** (adj.): richly colourful, attractive, dazzling.
   The Queen was **resplendent** in a rich gown and jewels at her coronation.

6. **Miscreant** (n.): someone who has broken the law, criminal, culprit, villain.
   Lawyers are doing their utmost to bring the **miscreant** to justice.

7. **Contrive** (v.): to bring about, engineer, plot.
   Lara **contrived** a routine where she could wake up late and still walk into class just before the bell rang.

8. **Corrupt** (adj.): immoral, dishonest, fraudulent; infected with a bug, unusable (of a computer).
   The new Prime Minister faced the huge challenge of trying to restructure the **corrupt** police force.

9. **Fickle** (adj.): frequently changing loyalties or affections; changeable, volatile.
   Hilary can be very **fickle**, and changes friendship groups every week.

10. **Purify** (v.): to decontaminate, cleanse, clean.
    On our camping trip, Mum told us to **purify** the water we took from the river because it was not clean enough to drink.

Exercise A: Synonyms

Write the word from the vocab list which is *most similar* in meaning next to each word listed below.

1. Engineer _____

2. Dazzling _____

3. Charity _____

4. Pale white _____

5. Referee _____

6. Lawbreaker_____

7. Changeable_____

8. Immoral _____

9. Decontaminate_____

10. Extremist _____

Exercise B: Complete the sentence

Write the most suitable word from the vocab list in the spaces below. You might need to change the form of the word; for instance, walk might become walked.

1. The charity was accused of being _____ after it was discovered that employees were stealing the public's donations.

2. Most crooks and _____s will end up in prison unless they change their ways.

3. The bride was _____ in her white gown, which was studded with tiny crystals.

4. Mum said fashion is _____ because last year skinny jeans were popular and this year everyone is wearing flares.

5. Daisy was very wealthy but generous, and known for her _____

6. Without a professional referee to _____, the Rugby World Cup Final could not take place.

7. Somehow Dad _____d to obtain tickets for the sold-out film premiere.

8. My brother says I am a video game _____ because I could play all day long.

9. The _____ cat has gorgeous white fur and pink eyes.

10. People believe that by washing in the mystical lake, they will _____ their minds and bodies.

Exercise C: Complete the sentence

Select the most suitable word from the choices provided.

1. Musa managed to _____ a fascinating story for his English homework.

    a. albino   **b. contrive**   **c. resplendent**

2. My uncle is currently training to _____ at our team's cricket matches.

    a. fanatic   **b. miscreant**   **c. officiate**

3. I bought a new filter that can _____ tap water, removing minerals and salts.

    a. corrupt   **b. purify**   **c. philanthropy**

4. It is hard to guess what Noah is thinking, as he is _____ and changes his mind all the time.

    a. fickle   **b. albino**   **c. officiate**

5. Charlie is a darts _____ and he plays matches every week.

    a. fanatic   **b. miscreant**   **c. contrive**

6. The calm sea was a deep, _____ blue in the afternoon sunshine.

    a. miscreant   **b. corrupt**   **c. resplendent**

7. Bill Gates gives much of his wealth to good causes and is famous for his _____.

    a. albino   **b. contrive**   **c. philanthropy**

8. The computer engineer realised that the new software he had installed was _____.

    a. corrupt   **b. fickle**   **c. officiate**

9. The teacher told us that if the _____ who was responsible for the graffiti did not own up then we would all stay in at break.

    a. fanatic   **b. miscreant**   **c. purify**

10. The unusual _____ lizard was hard to spot in its habitat on the white sand.

    a. contrive   **b. albino**   **c. resplendent**

Vocabulary 15

Learn the words below and then answer the questions that follow!

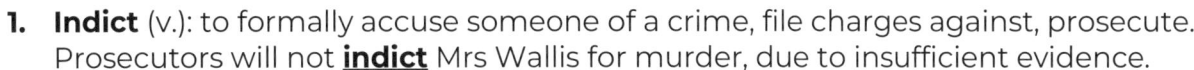

1. **Indict** (v.): to formally accuse someone of a crime, file charges against, prosecute.
    Prosecutors will not **indict** Mrs Wallis for murder, due to insufficient evidence.

2. **Perceptive** (adj.): observant, sensitive, insightful.
    The book was full of **perceptive** insights into philosophy, meaning that the readers learned a great deal.

3. **Bailiff** (n.): an official who confiscates someone's possessions if they owe money and cannot repay their debt, a debt-collector.
    Tom could not pay his rent, so his landlord sent over the **bailiff** to evict him from the house.

4. **Obnoxious** (adj.): unpleasant, rude, offensive, repulsive.
    Penny did not enjoy her first week at work because her boss was highly **obnoxious** and annoyed everyone.

5. **Genetic** (adj.): relating to genes and biology of heritable traits and characteristics.
    Asthma has a **genetic** cause but can be aggravated by pollution and pollen in the air.

6. **Prestigious** (adj.): highly respected, admired, reputable.
    The Oscars are arguably the most **prestigious** film awards, so to be nominated is a significant achievement.

7. **Impoverished** (adj.): very poor, disadvantaged, penniless.
    Throughout his **impoverished** childhood, Oliver had little money and few treats.

8. **Semblance** (n.): outward appearance, façade, front, pretence.
    Although I was nervous in my interview, I managed to project a **semblance** of confidence when I answered the questions.

9. **Delusion** (n.): false idea, mistaken impression, misconception, deception.
    Many students were under the **delusion** that the school would close when it snowed, however classes continued.

10. **Ardent** (adj.): very enthusiastic, passionate, avid.
    Sienna is an **ardent** nature lover who spends time outdoors whenever possible.

Exercise A: Synonyms

Write the word from the vocab list which is *most similar* in meaning next to each word listed below.

1. Respected _____

2. Avid _____

3. Debt-collector_____

4. Penniless _____

5. Inherited _____

6. Deception _____

7. Prosecute _____

8. Insightful _____

9. Offensive _____

10. Façade _____

VOCAB 15 WORD BANK

Indict

Perceptive

Bailiff

Obnoxious

Genetic

Prestigious

Impoverished

Semblance

Delusion

Ardent

Exercise B: Complete the sentence

Write the most suitable word from the vocab list in the spaces below. You might need to change the form of the word; for instance, walk might become walked.

1. Zubin was warned that if he did not pay his debt, the _____ would return.

2. Millie's skin disease is a _____ condition shared by many members of her family.

3. The _____ peasants wore rags and lived in tumbledown huts.

4. When Maureen is in a bad mood, she is _____ to everyone.

5. The disorganised group were under the _____ that they would finish first.

6. Donald is an _____ lover of Shakespeare and knows all the most famous quotations.

7. Detectives need to be incredibly _____ and sharp to crack tough cases.

8. Tom was a leading heart surgeon at the most _____ hospital in London.

9. There must be some _____ of order in a classroom if the children are to learn.

10. The jury is expected to _____ the woman for theft, because the evidence is clear.

Exercise C: Complete the sentence

Select the most suitable word from the choices provided.

1. The _____ tutor noticed that the little girl was struggling with her sums.

   a. indict   **b. perceptive**   **c. obnoxious**

2. Top companies want to hire students from the most _____ universities.

   a. bailiff   **b. semblance**   **c. prestigious**

3. After playing a minor role in the school production, Holly was under the _____ that she was on her way to stardom.

   a. genetic   **b. delusion**   **c. impoverished**

4. Kate was an _____ supporter of environmental initiatives such as tree planting.

   a. ardent   **b. obnoxious**   **c. perceptive**

5. The city returned to a _____ of normality after the wild New Year's celebrations.

   a. semblance   **b. prestigious**   **c. bailiff**

6. After the riots in town, the police arrested and _____ed five people.

   a. perceptive   **b. indict**   **c. delusion**

7. Many people found themselves rather _____ after a major bank went bust.

   a. ardent   **b. genetic**   **c. impoverished**

8. Luckily the old man paid his gambling debts before a _____ was sent to reclaim the money.

   a. bailiff   **b. semblance**   **c. prestigious**

9. Cristian's colleagues don't like working with him because he is _____ and loud.

   a. delusion   **b. ardent**   **c. obnoxious**

10. Saskia was fascinated by _____ biology, especially with eye colour variance.

    a. genetic   **b. indict**   **c. perceptive**

Vocabulary 16

Learn the words below and then answer the questions that follow!

1. **Propaganda** (n.): information, promotion or publicity which is exaggerated or intended to mislead, misinformation.
   Dictators have often used **propaganda** to convince the public of their corrupt policies.

2. **Abominable** (adj.): revolting, detestable, hateful, despicable.
   Despite the **abominable** weather, we had a great holiday in Wales.

3. **Poignant** (adj.): moving, touching, sad, heart-breaking.
   The **poignant** movie told a story of a painful childhood and the hero's unlikely success.

4. **Acquaintance** (n.): a person you know slightly, someone familiar, associate.
   Dave seemed to have more **acquaintances** than close friends; nobody knew him very well.

5. **Actuality** (n.): reality, in actual fact, in real life.
   The journey felt like a lifetime but in **actuality** it only lasted 5 hours.

6. **Delirious** (adj.): feverish, incoherent, wild, frenzied.
   The tropical heat rendered Ben **delirious** and confused, so he became lost on his trek through the jungle.

7. **Domain** (n.): an area or territory controlled by a particular ruler; realm, kingdom.
   King Harold built his castle on a hill so that he could survey his entire **domain**.

8. **Aristocracy** (n.): nobility, upper class, high society.
   For hundreds of years in Britain, the **aristocracy** controlled the government and ran the country.

9. **Contingent** (adj.): dependent upon, conditional.
   Dad's boss says his pay rise is **contingent** on the company doing well.

10. **Caricature** (n.): a picture, a light-hearted mocking representation of someone, a cartoon.
    A street artist drew a **caricature** of me, which depicted me with a huge nose and chin.

Exercise A: Synonyms

Write the word from the vocab list which is *most similar* in meaning next to each word listed below.

1. Reality _____

2. Incoherent _____

3. Nobility _____

4. Despicable _____

5. Cartoon _____

6. Moving _____

7. Misinformation _____

8. Dependent _____

9. Associate _____

10. Territory _____

Exercise B: Complete the sentence

Write the most suitable word from the vocab list in the spaces below. You might need to change the form of the word; for instance, walk might become walked.

1. The photo of her wedding dress brought back _____ memories for Amy.

2. Although stars in the sky seem tiny, in _____ they are much larger than Earth.

3. The free cheeseburger was _____ upon buying the meal deal first.

4. Brian said, "Happy to make your _____, Mr Turner."

5. The cat slaughtered a nest of baby birds in one act of _____ violence.

6. Tom felt _____ with exhaustion after completing his first marathon.

7. Robins are territorial and attack other birds in their _____.

8. Traditionally, hunting and shooting are pastimes associated with the _____.

9. Many artists and cartoonists draw hilarious _____s of politicians.

10. It is often hard to separate facts from _____ when researching the news on the internet.

Exercise C: Complete the sentence

Select the most suitable word from the choices provided.

1. Mrs Price says she does not cook at home because the kitchen is her husband's

    _____.

    a. aristocracy   **b. domain**   **c. caricature**

2. Tilly's new suit looked just as good in _____ as it did in the magazine.

    a. propaganda   **b. poignant**   **c. actuality**

3. On first _____ Dani seems friendly, but I haven't worked with her closely yet.

    a. contingent   **b. delirious**   **c. acquaintance**

4. Conor had _____ table manners: he slurped and burped throughout dinner!

    a. poignant   **b. aristocracy**   **c. abominable**

5. During World War II, the British government distributed _____ to encourage

    people to support the war effort.

    a. domain   **b. propaganda**   **c. acquaintance**

6. Lisa found her daughter's graduation ceremony moving and _____.

    a. poignant   **b. contingent**   **c. abominable**

7. Many large houses and country estates are still owned by the English _____.

    a. aristocracy   **b. delirious**   **c. actuality**

8. Getting into university is _____ upon obtaining good results in my A Levels.

    a. domain   **b. contingent**   **c. caricature**

9. The patient was suffering from a tropical bug which caused him to feel _____,

    with a high temperature.

    a. delirious   **b. aristocracy**   **c. acquaintance**

10. Morty's teacher was offended by the _____ drawn on the whiteboard.

    a. contingent   **b. poignant**   **c. caricature**

Vocabulary 17

Learn the words below and then answer the questions that follow!

1. **Insipid** (adj.): lacking flavour or taste, bland, dull, boring.
    Teddy claims he is an excellent chef but his curries are **insipid** and need more chilli.

2. **Imperative** (adj.): of vital importance, crucial, critical, essential.
    It was **imperative** that Luke left the restaurant in time to catch the last train home.

3. **Fraught** (adj.): full of or rife with something negative or problematic.
    The launch of the new app was **fraught** with setbacks due to software failures.

4. **Sentient** (adj.): able to feel or perceive things, living.
    Some robots are so advanced that they appear to be **sentient** lifeforms.

5. **Perverse** (adj.): deliberately unreasonable, wrong, obstructive, irrational.
    The selfish politician's **perverse** demands for an expensive new office were rejected by members of the public.

6. **Allay** (v.): to reduce, put to rest, calm, relieve, alleviate.
    The school's plans for a new building were supposed to **allay** fears of overcrowding in classrooms.

7. **Cavity** (n.): an empty space within a solid object; a hollow, nook.
    The ancient Egyptians stored the tombs of the Pharaohs in **cavities** within the pyramids.

8. **Salient** (adj.): outstanding, important, principal, main.
    Mina's presentation outlined all the **salient** issues of the topic to the class, leaving the detail to be covered by Juliet.

9. **Compensation** (n.): payment given to a victim, recompense, reimbursement.
    Mrs Jolly demanded **compensation** after the lorry drove into her garden wall and it needed rebuilding.

10. **Cosmos** (n.): the universe, outer space, the heavens.
    Lisa was given a telescope for her birthday to help develop her interest in space and the **cosmos**.

Exercise A: Synonyms

Write the word from the vocab list which is *most similar* in meaning next to each word listed below.

1. Hollow _____

2. Principal _____

3. Problematic_____

4. Recompense_____

5. Bland _____

6. Universe _____

7. Essential _____

8. Living _____

9. Relieve _____

10. Irrational _____

> ### VOCAB 17 WORD BANK
> Insipid
> Imperative
> Fraught
> Sentient
> Perverse
> Allay
> Cavity
> Salient
> Compensation
> Cosmos

Exercise B: Complete the sentence

Write the most suitable word from the vocab list in the spaces below. You might need to change the form of the word; for instance, walk might become walked.

1. After the accident, the insurance company granted Amy millions in _____.

2. Sailing in a storm can be _____ with difficulties if you are inexperienced.

3. The astronauts did not expect to find _____ creatures living on Mars.

4. I tried my utmost to _____ Tom's anxiety before his driving test.

5. Carlos found a childish and _____ enjoyment in annoying other people.

6. It is _____ that we find a strategy to beat the rival team.

7. I lost my ring in the _____ between the car seat and the gearstick.

8. The commentator said the team gave a dull and _____ performance last weekend against Manchester City.

9. My mind struggled to grasp the _____ points made in the teacher's talk.

10. One day, the human race may explore the farthest reaches of the _____.

Exercise C: Complete the sentence

Select the most suitable word from the choices provided.

1. The professor helped to _____ the students' fears when he told them exactly what would be in their test.

    a. salient   **b. allay**   **c. compensation**

2. The dentist said that the _____ in my tooth would need a filling.

    a. cavity   **b. cosmos**   **c. insipid**

3. Dan said he loved all _____ creatures, including snakes and cockroaches!

    a. fraught   **b. sentient**   **c. perverse**

4. Mum's doctor told her it was _____ that she stopped eating nuts as she had developed an allergy to them.

    a. cosmos   **b. allay**   **c. imperative**

5. Our guide led us down a route which was _____ with danger and I wanted to turn back.

    a. fraught   **b. cavity**   **c. perverse**

6. Across the _____ there are millions of galaxies, and possibly other lifeforms.

    a. cosmos   **b. perverse**   **c. insipid**

7. Unfortunately, my cousin was not entitled to any _____ after his fall at work.

    a. fraught   **b. allay**   **c. compensation**

8. The architect pointed out the _____ design features of the new building.

    a. cavity   **b. cosmos**   **c. salient**

9. Tim's _____ performance on stage failed to capture the audience's imagination.

    a. insipid   **b. imperative**   **c. compensation**

10. It was _____ of my sister to buy me a hot dog when I had asked for ice cream.

    a. allay   **b. perverse**   **c. fraught**

Vocabulary 18

Learn the words below and then answer the questions that follow!

1. **Remonstrate** (v.): to make a forceful protest, complain, oppose.
   Louisa **remonstrated** against claims that she had misused school funds by showing last year's bank statements.

2. **Satire** (n.): the use of humour, irony and exaggeration to criticise the stupidity of others, particularly in politics; mockery, parody.
   The newspaper published a **satire** that mocked the new government.

3. **Epidemic** (n.): a widespread outbreak of an infectious disease; crisis, plague.
   The NHS battled to contain the spread of the flu **epidemic**.

4. **Cremate** (v.): to burn (a body into ashes for a funeral service), incinerate.
   My grandfather wants to be **cremated** instead of buried when he passes away.

5. **Flagship** (n.): the best or most important thing or store owned by a company; focal point; the main ship of a fleet.
   The naval commander boarded the **flagship** and it prepared to set sail.

6. **Hiatus** (n.): a break, pause, interval, time out.
   After a brief **hiatus**, the two enemies resumed talks.

7. **Escapade** (n.): something involving excitement, adventure, exploit, antics.
   The students had some exciting **escapades** abroad during their gap year before university.

8. **Destitute** (adj.): extremely poor, poverty-stricken, penniless.
   The millionaire was left **destitute** and homeless after the collapse of his business.

9. **Pedantic** (adj.): extremely concerned with minor details, fussy, precise.
   When the teacher covered my essay in corrections, I felt he was being very **pedantic**.

10. **Extricate** (v.): to free, get out of, release, let loose, disconnect.
    Jack managed to **extricate** himself from looking after his younger siblings in order to go to the party.

Exercise A: Synonyms

Write the word from the vocab list which is *most similar* in meaning next to each word listed below.

1. Burn   _____

2. Precise   _____

3. Interval   _____

4. Mockery   _____

5. Penniless   _____

6. Plague   _____

7. Release   _____

8. Main store   _____

9. Adventure   _____

10. Protest   _____

Exercise B: Complete the sentence

Write the most suitable word from the vocab list in the spaces below. You might need to change the form of the word; for instance, walk might become walked.

1. Despite growing up virtually _____, Chris became very rich and successful.

2. There are fears that a yellow fever _____ could spread to the UK.

3. People say I am being _____ when I insist on being called Cassandra instead of Cassie.

4. Katy's Instagram followers love to see photos of her mountaineering _____s.

5. The lawyers managed to _____ their client from jail.

6. The retailer John Lewis has its _____ store on Oxford Street in London.

7. Mum _____d with the neighbours after they left rubbish bags all over our drive.

8. Tom is writing a _____ about the modern obsession with social media.

9. Dad managed to _____ all the sausages on the barbecue, leaving them charred and inedible.

10. After a five-year _____ the band re-formed and produced a new album.

Exercise C: Complete the sentence

Select the most suitable word from the choices provided.

1. The movie was a clever _____ of the fashion industry.

    a. hiatus   b. destitute   c. satire

2. My brother's latest _____ was to run away from boarding school and catch a boat to France.

    a. pedantic   b. escapade   c. epidemic

3. Dad _____d with the boys when they walked through the house with their muddy rugby boots on.

    a. extricate   b. cremate   c. remonstrate

4. We felt sorry for the _____ old man who was sleeping in a shop doorway.

    a. destitute   b. flagship   c. pedantic

5. The company will resume production of the car today after a six-month _____.

    a. satire   b. hiatus   c. escapade

6. The Spanish flu _____ after World War I killed millions of people worldwide.

    a. cremate   b. epidemic   c. remonstrate

7. "I don't mean to be _____, but can you please sweep up the crumbs from the floor?"

    a. pedantic   b. destitute   c. extricate

8. The fashion retailer's _____ in New York brings in more money than all the other shops put together.

    a. satire   b. escapade   c. flagship

9. In some cultures, the dead must always be _____d instead of buried.

    a. cremate   b. pedantic   c. hiatus

10. I wanted to _____ myself from the awkward situation but saw no escape.

    a. destitute   b. epidemic   c. extricate

Vocabulary 19

Learn the words below and then answer the questions that follow!

1. **Latent** (adj.): concealed, underlying, dormant, unseen.
    The **latent** tension between the two siblings boiled over when Luna borrowed her sister's jumper without asking.

2. **Emission** (n.): the sending out of gas, heat or light, release, production, discharge.
    Politicians want to drastically reduce **emissions** of CO2 which are damaging to the atmosphere.

3. **Hyperbole** (n.): exaggerated statements, excess, embellishment.
    You can't trust Jim's stories because he always uses **hyperbole** and massively exaggerates the truth.

4. **Fortitude** (n.): courage, resilience, strength.
    Although they were outnumbered, the soldiers had the **fortitude** to carry on fighting.

5. **Felony** (n.): A serious crime that can be punished by prison; offence.
    Arson, robbery and dangerous driving are amongst the most serious **felonies**.

6. **Bereft** (adj.): left without, lonely, abandoned, deprived.
    Mr Marner felt utterly **bereft** when his two daughters left home for university.

7. **Bide** (v.): to wait for, sit tight, withstand, tolerate.
    Clemence secretly wanted the top job but knew he would have to **bide** his time working as a junior assistant.

8. **Contravene** (v.): to break a law or a rule; violate, breach.
    Henry **contravened** school rules by being rude to the teacher and was punished with a Saturday detention.

9. **Drudgery** (n.): hard and boring work, labour, chores.
    Rachel found washing dishes at the cafe to be pure **drudgery**, so she decided to quit.

10. **Coalesce** (v.): to combine, merge, blend, join together.
    The tiny bubbles of gas **coalesced** into larger ones as they rose up the test tube.

Exercise A: Synonyms

Write the word from the vocab list which is *most similar* in meaning next to each word listed below.

1. Abandoned _____
2. Excess _____
3. Offence _____
4. Violate _____
5. Discharge _____
6. Resilience _____
7. Withstand _____
8. Combine _____
9. Dormant _____
10. Chore _____

VOCAB 19 WORD BANK

Latent

Emission

Hyperbole

Fortitude

Felony

Bereft

Bide

Contravene

Drudgery

Coalesce

Exercise B: Complete the sentence

Write the most suitable word from the vocab list in the spaces below. You might need to change the form of the word; for instance, walk might become walked.

1. The interviewer asked Hana to be truthful and to avoid _____ in her statement.

2. Phil loved going on holiday to escape the _____ of his everyday life.

3. The overcrowded stadium put many lives at risk and _____d safety laws.

4. The two streams _____ at the estuary and from there flow into the sea.

5. Harry decided to _____ his time until he had the chance to talk to Oskar alone.

6. The mechanic identified the source of gas _____s in the engine.

7. The empty streets seemed _____ of life after the hurricane.

8. To be successful you have to show _____ in the face of failure.

9. The summer course aimed to develop the _____ musical talent that Jeff believed all children possessed.

10. The accused has been charged with burglary and conspiracy to commit a further _____.

Exercise C: Complete the sentence

Select the most suitable word from the choices provided.

1. The campaign group proved that toxic _____s from the factory had poisoned local rivers.

    a. drudgery   **b. emission**   **c. contravene**

2. The weatherman said it was not _____ to call it the worst storm in 20 years.

    a. bereft   **b. felony**   **c. hyperbole**

3. The butter and oil began to melt and _____ together in the hot frying pan.

    a. coalesce   **b. bide**   **c. fortitude**

4. The chicken pox virus remained _____ in Sathnam's body, although he never showed symptoms.

    a. emission   **b. hyperbole**   **c. latent**

5. Kelly was totally _____ of confidence after she lost three tennis matches in a row.

    a. drudgery   **b. bereft**   **c. inhibit**

6. The unauthorised sale of films that have been pirated _____s many laws.

    a. contravene   **b. emission**   **c. fortitude**

7. Joe was charged with a _____, and went to prison for two years.

    a. felony   **b. hyperbole**   **c. coalesce**

8. The hospital cleaner found the _____ of scrubbing endless floors exhausting and boring.

    a. latent   **b. drudgery**   **c. bereft**

9. Despite being very small, Alex showed _____ and stood up to the school bully, so he was never bothered again.

    a. fortitude   **b. emission**   **c. contravene**

10. We decided to _____ our time and wait for the right moment to escape from the bandits.

    a. hyperbole   **b. coalesce**   **c. bide**

Vocabulary 20

Learn the words below and then answer the questions that follow!

1. **Grotesque** (adj.): shockingly ugly, distorted, horrifying, deformed.
   At Halloween, Charlotte dressed as Frankenstein's monster and wore a **grotesque** and scary mask.

2. **Absolve** (v.): to declare free from guilt or punishment, acquit, forgive, pardon.
   It is said that "time heals", meaning that time can **absolve** us of mistakes or help us forget them.

3. **Reticent** (adj.): holding back emotions, reserved, shy, withdrawn.
   Mark was a **reticent** young boy who did not like to answer questions about himself.

4. **Allude** (v.): to call attention to, hint at, imply, suggest.
   Many of Wordsworth's poems contain imagery that **alludes** to the significance of childhood.

5. **Primal** (adj.): early stage of human development; primeval, most important, primary, fundamental.
   Biologists believe that we are almost genetically identical to our **primal** ancestors from many thousands of years ago.

6. **Disinherit** (v.): to cut someone out of one's will; to dispossess, cut off.
   Adele's parents said they would **disinherit** her if she continued to get in trouble with the police.

7. **Predatory** (adj.): exploiting or preying on others; carnivorous, hunting.
   Tiger sharks are a **predatory** species, hunting a wide range of other creatures including fish, seals and squid.

8. **Hound** (v.): to harass, pursue relentlessly, pester.
   Eliza **hounded** her father to take her to Disneyland Paris until he finally gave in.

9. **Meteoric** (adj.): relating to meteors; very rapid, swift, quick.
   The singer had a **meteoric** rise to fame after releasing her first album.

10. **Beseech** (v.): to plead with, implore, beg.
    The knight fell at the queen's feet and **beseeched** her to spare his life.

Exercise A: Synonyms

Write the word from the vocab list which is *most similar* in meaning next to each word listed below.

1. Rapid _____

2. Dispossess _____

3. Withdrawn _____

4. Carnivorous_____

5. Acquit _____

6. Imply _____

7. Implore _____

8. Deformed _____

9. Primary _____

10. Harass _____

Exercise B: Complete the sentence

Write the most suitable word from the vocab list in the spaces below. You might need to change the form of the word; for instance, walk might become walked.

1. We did not know exactly why Florence was upset but she did _____ to the fact that we had gone out without her.

2. Nico is quite _____ and dislikes having to socialise at parties or events.

3. Lord Stanmore said he would _____ his daughter for marrying a bank robber.

4. The charity worked to _____ the imprisoned journalist of all wrongdoing.

5. I _____ you to help me with this project so that we can both go home early.

6. When the lion approached, our _____ instinct was to run for our lives!

7. If you stop _____ing me, then I may be more inclined to do the washing up!

8. Tim showed us _____ photos of his broken leg, in which it was twisted round the wrong way.

9. Mike was a _____ individual who always took advantage of his friends.

10. Apple has experienced _____ growth since it launched the first iPhone.

Exercise C: Complete the sentence

Select the most suitable word from the choices provided.

1. If the prisoner is not _____d of his crime, he will face the death penalty.

   a. hound   **b. absolve**   **c. reticent**

2. Ishmael had a _____, instinctive fear of spiders and snakes.

   a. primal   **b. meteoric**   **c. grotesque**

3. The _____ businessman extracted thousands of pounds from the charity.

   a. disinherit   **b. predatory**   **c. hound**

4. Milo _____ed Fatima to help him solve the tricky maths questions.

   a. absolve   **b. allude**   **c. beseech**

5. Huge investments in Manchester City FC assisted their _____ rise to the top.

   a. primal   **b. allude**   **c. meteoric**

6. My mum thought that the horror film was too _____ for me to watch.

   a. reticent   **b. grotesque**   **c. predatory**

7. I don't think my parents would ever _____ me, because we are a very close family.

   a. absolve   **b. disinherit**   **c. primal**

8. The princess was _____ed by photographers every minute of the day.

   a. meteoric   **b. beseech**   **c. hound**

9. Many of the students were _____ about answering questions in class.

   a. reticent   **b. primal**   **c. grotesque**

10. Finlay is embarrassed about the large orange juice stain on his shirt, so please do not

    _____ to it when you see him.

    a. disinherit   **b. hound**   **c. allude**

Answers

Vocabulary 1

Exercise A

1. Morale
2. Replenish
3. Eligible
4. Conservatory
5. Mandatory
6. Secondary
7. Pitiless
8. Nausea
9. Analyse
10. Malignant

Exercise B

1. Mandatory
2. Pitiless
3. Nausea
4. Morale
5. Replenish
6. Analyse
7. Secondary
8. Eligible
9. Malignant
10. Conservatory

Exercise C

1. Eligible
2. Morale
3. Replenish
4. Nausea
5. Mandatory
6. Analyse
7. Secondary
8. Malignant
9. Pitiless
10. Conservatory

Vocabulary 2

Exercise A

1. Esteem
2. Flippant
3. Incessant
4. Parable
5. Feasible
6. Sympathise
7. Cumbersome
8. Indignation
9. Inquest
10. Aromatic

Exercise B

1. Indignation
2. Incessant
3. Feasible
4. Cumbersome
5. Esteem
6. Aromatic
7. Parable
8. Inquest
9. Flippant
10. Sympathise

Exercise C

1. Aromatic
2. Cumbersome
3. Parable
4. Feasible
5. Sympathise
6. Incessant
7. Indignation
8. Esteem
9. Inquest
10. Flippant

Vocabulary 3

Exercise A

1. Interject
2. Replete
3. Trite
4. Jeopardise
5. Administration
6. Hospitality
7. Thrifty
8. Stipulate
9. Delectable
10. Definite

Exercise B

1. Delectable
2. Administration
3. Interject
4. Thrifty
5. Stipulate
6. Definite
7. Trite
8. Jeopardise
9. Hospitality
10. Replete

Exercise C

1. Stipulate
2. Jeopardise
3. Trite
4. Definite
5. Delectable
6. Thrifty
7. Administration
8. Hospitality
9. Interject
10. Replete

Answers

Vocabulary 4

Exercise A

1. Enmity
2. Reduction
3. Grandeur
4. Orthodox
5. Consolidate
6. Tangible
7. Satisfaction
8. Undefined
9. Composed
10. Impede

Exercise B

1. Satisfaction
2. Tangible
3. Composed
4. Impede
5. Enmity
6. Reduction
7. Grandeur
8. Consolidate
9. Undefined
10. Orthodox

Exercise C

1. Impede
2. Consolidate
3. Composed
4. Satisfaction
5. Tangible
6. Orthodox
7. Undefined
8. Grandeur
9. Reduction
10. Enmity

Vocabulary 5

Exercise A

1. Shrewd
2. Prerequisite
3. Conspicuous
4. Deplete
5. Cohesive
6. Daunting
7. Acrid
8. Abhor
9. Assailant
10. Frugal

Exercise B

1. Acrid
2. Abhor
3. Assailant
4. Conspicuous
5. Prerequisite
6. Cohesive
7. Shrewd
8. Frugal
9. Deplete
10. Daunting

Exercise C

1. Frugal
2. Daunting
3. Shrewd
4. Prerequisite
5. Abhor
6. Acrid
7. Conspicuous
8. Assailant
9. Cohesive
10. Deplete

Vocabulary 6

Exercise A

1. Verification
2. Dilapidated
3. Hindrance
4. Empathy
5. Predicament
6. Gratuitous
7. Raucous
8. Resonate
9. Almanac
10. Preposterous

Exercise B

1. Resonate
2. Empathy
3. Verification
4. Gratuitous
5. Predicament
6. Hindrance
7. Raucous
8. Preposterous
9. Dilapidated
10. Almanac

Exercise C

1. Verification
2. Gratuitous
3. Dilapidated
4. Predicament
5. Almanac
6. Raucous
7. Preposterous
8. Resonate
9. Empathy
10. Hindrance

Vocabulary 7

Exercise A

1. Dehydrated
2. Sanction
3. Augment
4. Abdomen
5. Tedious
6. Admonish
7. Torrid
8. Exude
9. Invoke
10. Repugnant

Exercise B

1. Augment
2. Admonish
3. Tedious
4. Abdomen
5. Invoke
6. Exude
7. Repugnant
8. Dehydrated
9. Sanction
10. Torrid

Exercise C

1. Exude
2. Invoke
3. Abdomen
4. Repugnant
5. Tedious
6. Torrid
7. Admonish
8. Augment
9. Sanction
10. Dehydrated

Answers

Vocabulary 8

Exercise A

1. Linguist
2. Pacify
3. Mediocre
4. Recur
5. Bountiful
6. Rabid
7. Deplore
8. Brandish
9. Dissuade
10. Undeniable

Exercise B

1. Brandish
2. Mediocre
3. Dissuade
4. Linguist
5. Bountiful
6. Pacify
7. Undeniable
8. Recur
9. Rabid
10. Deplore

Exercise C

1. Linguist
2. Deplore
3. Pacify
4. Mediocre
5. Undeniable
6. Rabid
7. Dissuade
8. Recur
9. Brandish
10. Bountiful

Vocabulary 9

Exercise A

1. Canon
2. Parity
3. Transfusion
4. Stupendous
5. Suave
6. Tsunami
7. Ebony
8. Wield
9. Scrutiny
10. Eulogy

Exercise B

1. Eulogy
2. Wield
3. Tsunami
4. Suave
5. Stupendous
6. Transfusion
7. Canon
8. Scrutiny
9. Ebony
10. Parity

Exercise C

1. Tsunami
2. Wield
3. Stupendous
4. Transfusion
5. Canon
6. Suave
7. Ebony
8. Eulogy
9. Parity
10. Scrutiny

Vocabulary 10

Exercise A

1. Plagiarise
2. Subterranean
3. Diabolical
4. Centenary
5. Accountable
6. Tutelage
7. Thesis
8. Ultimatum
9. Vandalism
10. Atrocities

Exercise B

1. Centenary
2. Accountable
3. Atrocities
4. Plagiarise
5. Vandalism
6. Tutelage
7. Ultimatum
8. Subterranean
9. Thesis
10. Diabolical

Exercise C

1. Ultimatum
2. Vandalism
3. Plagiarise
4. Thesis
5. Subterranean
6. Tutelage
7. Diabolical
8. Atrocities
9. Centenary
10. Accountable

Vocabulary 11

Exercise A

1. Compensate
2. Vaccine
3. Telepathy
4. Rhapsody
5. Lucid
6. Transcend
7. Testify
8. Volition
9. Susceptible
10. Temperamental

Exercise B

1. Lucid
2. Telepathy
3. Susceptible
4. Volition
5. Transcend
6. Vaccine
7. Rhapsody
8. Testify
9. Compensate
10. Temperamental

Exercise C

1. Volition
2. Transcend
3. Temperamental
4. Lucid
5. Vaccine
6. Susceptible
7. Telepathy
8. Rhapsody
9. Compensate
10. Testify

Answers

Vocabulary 12

Exercise A

1. Conceited
2. Catalyst
3. Impervious
4. Rebuke
5. Armoury
6. Abundant
7. Sinew
8. Upheaval
9. Fluctuate
10. Tyrannical

Exercise B

1. Rebuke
2. Fluctuate
3. Tyrannical
4. Armoury
5. Impervious
6. Catalyst
7. Abundant
8. Upheaval
9. Sinew
10. Conceited

Exercise C

1. Upheaval
2. Armoury
3. Rebuke
4. Conceited
5. Tyrannical
6. Catalyst
7. Abundant
8. Sinew
9. Fluctuate
10. Impervious

Vocabulary 13

Exercise A

1. Inherent
2. Tolerance
3. Advocacy
4. Dismissive
5. Vigilant
6. Ostracise
7. Transfer
8. Tact
9. Adjourn
10. Risible

Exercise B

1. Transfer
2. Dismissive
3. Adjourn
4. Advocacy
5. Inherent
6. Ostracise
7. Risible
8. Tolerance
9. Vigilant
10. Tact

Exercise C

1. Adjourn
2. Vigilant
3. Dismissive
4. Risible
5. Inherent
6. Tolerance
7. Advocacy
8. Transfer
9. Tact
10. Ostracise

Vocabulary 14

Exercise A

1. Contrive
2. Resplendent
3. Philanthropy
4. Albino
5. Officiate
6. Miscreant
7. Fickle
8. Corrupt
9. Purify
10. Fanatic

Exercise B

1. Corrupt
2. Miscreant
3. Resplendent
4. Fickle
5. Philanthropy
6. Officiate
7. Contrive
8. Fanatic
9. Albino
10. Purify

Exercise C

1. Contrive
2. Officiate
3. Purify
4. Fickle
5. Fanatic
6. Resplendent
7. Philanthropy
8. Corrupt
9. Miscreant
10. Albino

Vocabulary 15

Exercise A

1. Prestigious
2. Ardent
3. Bailiff
4. Impoverished
5. Genetic
6. Delusion
7. Indict
8. Perceptive
9. Obnoxious
10. Semblance

Exercise B

1. Bailiff
2. Genetic
3. Impoverished
4. Obnoxious
5. Delusion
6. Ardent
7. Perceptive
8. Prestigious
9. Semblance
10. Indict

Exercise C

1. Perceptive
2. Prestigious
3. Delusion
4. Ardent
5. Semblance
6. Indict
7. Impoverished
8. Bailiff
9. Obnoxious
10. Genetic

Vocabulary 16

Exercise A

1. Actuality
2. Delirious
3. Aristocracy
4. Abominable
5. Caricature
6. Poignant
7. Propaganda
8. Contingent
9. Acquaintance
10. Domain

Exercise B

1. Poignant
2. Actuality
3. Contingent
4. Acquaintance
5. Abominable
6. Delirious
7. Domain
8. Aristocracy
9. Caricature
10. Propaganda

Exercise C

1. Domain
2. Actuality
3. Acquaintance
4. Abominable
5. Propaganda
6. Poignant
7. Aristocracy
8. Contingent
9. Delirious
10. Caricature

Vocabulary 17

Exercise A

1. Cavity
2. Salient
3. Fraught
4. Compensation
5. Insipid
6. Cosmos
7. Imperative
8. Sentient
9. Allay
10. Perverse

Exercise B

1. Compensation
2. Fraught
3. Sentient
4. Allay
5. Perverse
6. Imperative
7. Cavity
8. Insipid
9. Salient
10. Cosmos

Exercise C

1. Allay
2. Cavity
3. Sentient
4. Imperative
5. Fraught
6. Cosmos
7. Compensation
8. Salient
9. Insipid
10. Perverse

Answers

Vocabulary 18

Exercise A

1. Cremate
2. Pedantic
3. Hiatus
4. Satire
5. Destitute
6. Epidemic
7. Extricate
8. Flagship
9. Escapade
10. Remonstrate

Exercise B

1. Destitute
2. Epidemic
3. Pedantic
4. Escapade
5. Extricate
6. Flagship
7. Remonstrate
8. Satire
9. Cremate
10. Hiatus

Exercise C

1. Satire
2. Escapade
3. Remonstrate
4. Destitute
5. Hiatus
6. Epidemic
7. Pedantic
8. Flagship
9. Cremate
10. Extricate

Vocabulary 19

Exercise A

1. Bereft
2. Hyperbole
3. Felony
4. Contravene
5. Emission
6. Fortitude
7. Bide
8. Coalesce
9. Latent
10. Drudgery

Exercise B

1. Hyperbole
2. Drudgery
3. Contravene
4. Coalesce
5. Bide
6. Emission
7. Bereft
8. Fortitude
9. Latent
10. Felony

Exercise C

1. Emission
2. Hyperbole
3. Coalesce
4. Latent
5. Bereft
6. Contravene
7. Felony
8. Drudgery
9. Fortitude
10. Bide

Vocabulary 20

Exercise A

1. Meteoric
2. Disinherit
3. Reticent
4. Predatory
5. Absolve
6. Allude
7. Beseech
8. Grotesque
9. Primal
10. Hound

Exercise B

1. Allude
2. Reticent
3. Disinherit
4. Absolve
5. Beseech
6. Primal
7. Hound
8. Grotesque
9. Predatory
10. Meteoric

Exercise C

1. Absolve
2. Primal
3. Predatory
4. Beseech
5. Meteoric
6. Grotesque
7. Disinherit
8. Hound
9. Reticent
10. Allude